Where the Wild Things Learn!

Playing the W.I.L.D. Card: A School Leader's Guide to Understanding the Non-Conforming Student with Humor and Heart

Candice Vance Anderson

MPowerED Press

Published in the United States by MPowering Legacy Publishing, a sub-company of MPowering Legacy, LLC, Mississippi.

www.mpoweringlegacy.com

Dr. Candice Vance Anderson

Where the Wild Things Learn!: Playing the W.I.L.D. Card: A School Leader's Guide to Understanding the Non-Conforming Student with Humor and Heart

Version 1- June 3, 2025

Ebook ISBN:

Paperback ISBN:

Hardcover ISBN:

Manufactured in the United States of America.

Printed in the United States of America

Contents

Dedication

*F*or the ones who don't match the mold—but still move the mission. This one's for you.

Yeah, *you*—the educator who talks with their hands, colors outside the lines, and side-eyes every PD PowerPoint that starts with "Norms." The one who has been called *"too much," "too loud," "too creative,"* or *"not the right fit."* The one who brings snacks to IEP meetings, jokes to faculty trainings, and soul to sterile spaces.

This book is for the non-conforming personalities: the unicorns in khakis and the glitter under the radar. The ones who know that teaching is performance *and* ministry, classroom *and* comedy show, structure *and* soul.

You have been in rooms where your brilliance was misunderstood. Where your boldness made folks uncomfortable. Where your passion was *labeled* before it was celebrated.

But let me tell you this: You are not the problem—you are the *pattern disruptor.*

You are not "too much"—you are *exactly what's been missing.*

You've turned chaos into culture, confusion into curiosity, and routines into rituals.

You've made kids believe in themselves just by being yourself.

You've led with your gut when the guidebook fell short—and somehow, your classroom still felt like home.

So, to every teacher, leader, paraprofessional, parent, or student who ever dared to be a little *extra* in a world asking for *less*...

- May you never shrink to fit systems that weren't built for your brilliance.

- May you keep leading loud, laughing loud,and loving big.

- May this book remind you that *you* are not alone.

- You are a WILD card.

And baby, you were born to change the game!

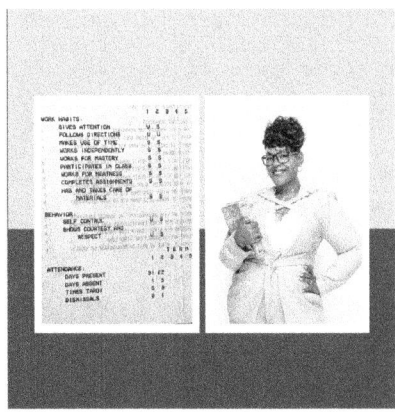

Preface

Before you even waste your time reading the next few pages, let me give you my outlook on education:

I believe that every individual, regardless of their background or circumstances, has an inherent right to be heard and to feel that their voice matters. This principle is not merely a guiding value—it is a foundational belief that drives my leadership and shapes my approach to education. When students, educators, and families feel heard and valued, they are empowered to engage fully, both academically and emotionally, creating a culture of trust, respect, and growth.

In education, the act of listening goes beyond hearing words; it involves recognizing the unique experiences, perspectives, and aspirations that each person brings to the table. When we create spaces where every voice counts, we foster a sense of belonging and purpose that enhances learning outcomes across all dimensions: academic, functional, and emotional.

Academically, students thrive when they feel respected and supported. By listening to their needs, concerns, and ideas, we can tailor learning experiences that are engaging, relevant, and challenging. This approach nurtures curiosity and encourages active participation, ensuring that students are not passive recipients of knowledge but active contributors to their educational journey. When students know that their thoughts and perspectives are valued, they are more likely to take ownership of their learning and strive for excellence.

Functionally, the power of listening and inclusion extends to the practical skills and strategies students need to succeed in life. By valuing their input, we help them build confidence in their decision-making abilities and problem-solving skills. Creating opportunities for collaboration and leadership allows students to see the impact of their contributions, preparing them to navigate complex systems and advocate for themselves and others in meaningful ways.

Emotionally, the simple act of being heard can transform a student's experience. Feeling seen and understood fosters emotional resilience, self-worth, and a willingness to take risks. In a world where many young people face challenges that threaten their sense of identity and belonging, it is essential to create environments where they feel safe to express themselves without fear of judgment. This emotional safety is a cornerstone for deeper connections and personal growth, enabling students to explore their potential and embrace their individuality.

For educators, families, and communities, this philosophy of inclusion and validation is equally impactful. Empowering teachers to voice their insights and ideas fosters innovation and professional growth. Engaging families as partners in the educational process builds trust and collaboration, ensuring that each student's needs are met holistically. Communities that prioritize listening create strong networks of support, where the collective vision for success becomes a shared responsibility.

As an educational leader, I am committed to modeling this philosophy in every aspect of my work. Whether mentoring aspiring leaders, collaborating with colleagues, or engaging with students, I strive to ensure that every person believes their voice matters. This commitment to inclusion and respect is not only a moral imperative but also a practical strategy for achieving excellence. When people feel heard, they are more willing to invest their energy, creativity, and passion into the shared mission of growth and achievement.

Ultimately, I believe that education is about more than imparting knowledge; it is about cultivating individuals who are confident, compassionate, and capable of making meaningful contributions to the world. By ensuring that every person feels heard and valued, we create a legacy of empowerment and leadership that transcends the classroom and transforms lives.

This is the essence of my philosophy and the guiding force behind my work as an educator and leader.

If you're reading this sentence, you may be a person in leadership trying fervently to understand how to lead those who seemingly march to the beat of their own drum.

If you made it to this sentence, you may be the parent of a child who certainly makes it known that they have their own idea of what success looks like for them, and unfortunately, it is not the path you would have created for them to walk.

If you make it to THIS sentence, you have begun to reflect. You have begun to wonder, like me, if you have simply been a victim of the perpetual cycle of judgment from leaders who will not take the time to understand that every one of us deserves to have a leader who values authenticity. Simply put, the check that an educator wrote me at age five, encouraging me that I could be "anything" I wanted to be if I just stayed focused and worked hard, I've come to cash in!

Some of my FAVORITE books and television shows incorporate the theme of the non-conforming thinker!

A Tale of Two Journeys: *Where the Wild Things Are* & *Quantum Leap*

At first glance, *Where the Wild Things Are,* the classic children's book by Maurice Sendak, and *Quantum Leap,* the sci-fi TV show about a time-traveling physicist, might seem to exist in entirely different universes. One is about a mischievous child escaping reality to rule over fantastical creatures, while the other follows a scientist who "leaps" into different bodies to correct historical wrongs. Yet, at their core, both stories revolve around transformation, adaptability, and the journey of self-discovery—themes that resonate deeply with non-conforming students.

The Common Thread: The Wild & The Wanderer

Both Max (*Where the Wild Things Are*) and Dr. Sam Beckett (*Quantum Leap*) are outsiders navigating unpredictable worlds. They don't fit into the expectations set for them, and instead of simply following the rules, they carve their own paths:

- Max is a defiant child, exiled to his room for misbehavior, who finds a portal to a land where he can be wild and free. Yet, despite becoming "king," he ultimately realizes that true belonging is not about ruling over chaos—it is about understanding oneself and finding balance.

- Sam Beckett is a scientist who, after an experiment gone wrong, jumps through time into other people's lives. His mission? To fix problems, right injustices, and help people understand their potential—all while searching for a way home.

Both characters represent the power of nonconformity—their refusal to accept the status quo leads them on transformative journeys where they use their unique perspectives to make meaningful changes.

Contrast: Impulsivity vs. Responsibility

While both Max and Sam are nonconformists, their approaches to problem-solving differ.

- Max's journey is emotional. He acts on impulse, driven by frustration, and initially revels in the freedom of chaos.

His adventure teaches him that leadership and independence require more than just rebellion—they require wisdom and responsibility.

- Sam's journey is intellectual. He is forced into situations beyond his control, yet he adapts quickly, using empathy, problem-solving, and knowledge to help people. He doesn't seek power but rather understanding and justice.

Relating to Non-conforming Students

Non-conforming students often resemble a mix of both characters. They reject traditional expectations, question authority, and struggle with imposed rules. Like Max, they may express their frustration through disruptive behaviors. Like Sam, they often see the world differently and seek meaning beyond the standard curriculum.

However, their greatest strength is also their potential: they don't just accept things "as they are." When guided properly, their ability to question, challenge, and think beyond conventional norms can lead to groundbreaking innovation, creative problem-solving, and leadership.

Harnessing Nonconformity for Growth & Innovation

Instead of trying to tame or "fix" non-conforming students, educators and leaders should channel their strengths into productive, meaningful outlets.

1. Problem-Solving & Leadership

- Just like Max learns that ruling the Wild Things isn't about control but about understanding and connection, non-conforming students can become excellent leaders when given responsibility and trust.

- Example: Student-Led Initiatives—Encourage them to run peer mentorship programs, lead community projects, or even design their own learning experiences.

2. Adaptability & Innovation

- Sam Beckett thrives because he adapts—a skill that non-conforming students naturally develop when they challenge the status quo.

- Example: Project-Based Learning—Instead of worksheets, let them solve real-world problems—create businesses, design solutions for community issues, or develop new school policies.

3. Embracing Curiosity & Creativity

- Max's wild imagination creates an entire world, while Sam's intellect finds solutions no one else can see.

- Example: Creative Expression & Technology Integration—Let students explore art, music, coding, and storytelling as ways to express their ideas and challenge norms.

The POINT? The Wild Becomes the Wise!

The wildness of Max and the adaptability of Sam Beckett reflect the strengths of non-conforming students. Instead of suppressing their energy, channel it into self-improvement, leadership skills, and effective problem-solving.

We realize the best schools and communities are not those that "tame" nonconformists—they are the ones that make space for wildness to evolve into wisdom. Because when students are given the chance to challenge, create, and lead, they don't just find where they belong—they build a future where everyone can thrive.

Introduction

Leadership in schools is an unpredictable game. You walk in with a playbook, but the "players"—students, teachers, parents—each bring their own strategies, personalities, and quirks. It's a bit like playing UNO with someone who makes up the rules as they go: you need to expect the unexpected.

This book is a survival guide for the school leader who finds themselves managing a wild kingdom. It's about navigating the chaos, taming the wild (while keeping its spirit intact), and making humor your most reliable ally. In a world where education often focuses on taming creativity and individuality, the true challenge is to let the wild flourish, structured by wisdom and strategy.

Together, we will explore:

Understanding Non-Conformity

We will delve into the philosophies of education pioneers like John Dewey and Howard Gardner to understand how to harness the wildness inherent in learning environments.

We will reintroduce ourselves to learning how Maslow's Hierarchy of Needs applies to creating a foundation of safety and belonging for non-conforming students AND staff.

The Power of Adaptability

Using the WILD Card Strategy, we will explore how flexibility can turn challenging situations into opportunities.

In addition, let's discover how Vygotsky's *Zone of Proximal Development* helps in setting growth targets that stretch but don't overwhelm.

Fostering Curiosity and Creativity

We will learn how to transform disruptive curiosity into productive learning by using Carol Dweck's growth mindset framework.

Then, we will explore Ken Robinson's principles of creativity and how humor and spontaneity can foster connection and innovation.

Building Community

How do we establish effective partnerships with parents using Epstein's Framework of Six Types of Involvement?

Once we have become partners, how can we develop a culture that embraces WILD and builds on collective strengths?

Guiding the Wild

Incorporating Paulo Freire's dialogic learning techniques to co-create knowledge and empower students and staff creates inclusive, student-centered initiatives where WILD learners of all ages thrive.

The Role of Humor in Leadership

Understand the psychology of laughter and its role in managing stress and fostering collaboration.

Develop strategies to use humor effectively as a de-escalation tool.

Each chapter will dive deep into these elements, blending anecdotes, actionable strategies, and expert insights. From taming the chaos of the classroom to navigating the dynamics of a parent-teacher conference, this guide equips school leaders to embrace the wildness and steer it toward success.

Let's just go ahead and put it out there: This ain't for the weak! Rest in that. It's ok.

Everybody does not have the temperance to deal with those of us who are nonconformists. That's right. I have labeled myself a NON-CONFORMIST. YOU would have labeled me stubborn, problematic, argumentative, and BAD! I was the straight-A student with Unsatisfactory Conduct. I was the student that, if told to walk in a straight line, YEARNED to zig-zag.

And here I sit. A Doctoral Degree earning, wife and mother of a blended family of four, KILLING THE EDUCATION GAME! Do YOU know why? It's plain and simple.

I believe that our individual embrace of who we authentically are paves the way for our individual success. I have learned that schools and teachers do not always know how to support non-traditional learners because the system is set up to do nothing BUT conform.

Nevertheless, people—nonconformists, if embraced and respectfully guided—are CHANGE AGENTS! We're problem solvers. We're Climate and Culture specialists. We're capable of fear, but our fierce overcoming personality creates opportunities to push against the status quo! We're the PERFECT wild card, but ONLY if you know how to strategize.

In this book, I will use "W.I.L.D." and "Nonconforming" interchangeably. Let's define.

Definition of a Non-conformist Student

A non-conformist student is one who resists traditional norms, expectations, and conventional ways of thinking, learning, and behaving in the classroom. Unlike students who are oppositional or disruptive for defiant reasons, non-conformist students push boundaries not out of disrespect but rather from curiosity, creativity, or a desire to challenge the status quo. They are often critical thinkers, independent learners, and innovators who may struggle with rigid rules and structured environments.

Key Characteristics of Non-conformist Students

- Curious & Questioning: They frequently challenge authority or classroom rules not to rebel but to understand the rationale behind them.

- Creative & Independent Thinkers: They enjoy experimenting with new ideas and may not follow traditional problem-solving methods.

- Resistant to Authority (But Not Defiant): They dislike arbitrary rules and will push back if something seems unfair or unnecessary.

- Highly Individualistic: They prefer to express themselves in unique ways, whether in learning, dress, or behavior.

- Innovative Problem-Solvers: They may see multiple solutions to a problem and resist being confined to one approach.

- Non-Traditional Learners: They may struggle in environments that prioritize rote memorization and rigid structures.

- Strong Sense of Justice & Ethics: They often advocate for fairness and equality, even if it challenges authority figures.

Examples of Non-conformist Student Behaviors

1. A student refuses to complete an assignment in the traditional format (e.g., instead of a written essay, they want to create a video presentation).

2. A student constantly asks "why" regarding classroom rules, grading policies, or societal norms.

3. A student dresses in a way that stands out (e.g., wearing unconventional clothing, accessories, or hairstyles that go against school trends).

Now, I know by now, you are either feeling excited and "seen" or you are saying to yourself, "Who the hell has time to deal with that in an eight-hour day?" YOU! Lol! You've got to deal with it one way or another. Why not find ways to embrace this challenge and show this student (and most likely others you work with) how people with differences have just as much of a place in this world as those who have polar opposite responses?

Enough chatter! Let's dive in!

Why Do Some Students Choose to Non-conform?

Not all nonconformists are the same—some challenge the system for intellectual reasons, others out of frustration, and some just because they see the world differently. Understanding *why* a student resists conformity is the first step in supporting them effectively.

1. They See Things Differently

Some students simply have a unique way of thinking. Traditional classroom norms—sit still, take notes, follow instructions—may not align with their natural learning style.

Example: A student who doodles during a lecture is not being defiant—this might help them process information better.

2. They Crave Autonomy

Non-conformist students often resist authority not out of defiance but because they feel more engaged when they have control over their choices.

Example: Instead of being told exactly how to write an essay, they might prefer to turn it into a podcast or video.

3. They Challenge Injustice or Hypocrisy (This is a BIG one for me!)

Many nonconformists are deep thinkers who notice flaws in systems. They may speak out against unfair rules or outdated traditions.

Example: A high school student protests that a dress code unfairly targets girls, leading a campaign for change.

4. They Are Driven by Passion, Not Structure

Some students resist traditional schooling because it does not align with their passions. They may struggle to engage with subjects that do not interest them, but they will hyper-focus on topics they love.

Example: A student who refuses to complete math homework might spend hours coding their own video game at home.

5. They Enjoy Being Playful & Pushing Boundaries (Here's where you want to QUIT!)

Some kids are just natural jokers—not to be malicious, but because they enjoy pushing boundaries to see what happens.

Example: When asked to describe themselves in one word on an assignment, they write *anti-disestablishmentarianism* just to see if the teacher will react.

Non-conformist students are not problems to be fixed—they are future leaders, artists, innovators, and change-makers.

By creating a classroom and home environment that values curiosity, critical thinking, and individual expression, we don't just make school more engaging for them—we prepare them to change the world!

Chapter 1
The Principal's Wild Kingdom

When I was first allowed to wear the school leader's hat, I imagined myself as the fearless captain of a mighty educational ship. Turns out, I was more like a zookeeper. From the moment I walked into the building, it was clear: students were not the only "wild cards" in this game. Teachers, parents, and yes, even the occasional central office staff member were wild cards—everyone had their moments of uncontainable chaos.

The Cafeteria Conundrum

Principal Seals, a veteran leader, thought she had seen it all—until Taco Tuesday turned into a school-wide food fight that rivaled an action movie scene. As she ducked behind a trash can to avoid an airborne burrito, she grabbed the microphone and announced, "Ladies and gentlemen, welcome to our new student-led initiative, The Great Guacamole Games. The winner gets to clean up!" Instantly, the chaos ceased, and students frantically searched for mops instead of nacho cheese ammunition.

The Great Kindergarten Stampede

Mrs. Kelly, the assistant principal, was proud of her well-rehearsed morning routine—until a kindergartener discovered that his new light-up sneakers made a "cool noise" when he ran. Like dominoes, an entire class of five-year-olds took off, creating a stampede reminiscent of an elementary version of *The Lion King*. Mrs. Kelly, thinking quickly, grabbed a whistle and shouted, "Alright, you wild stallions! First one to trot calmly gets a sticker!" With the promise of a sticker (obviously the currency of power in K-2), order was restored.

The Case of the Copy Machine Catastrophe

Assistant Principal White entered the teacher's lounge to find Mrs. Polk, the science teacher, staring at the copy machine as though it had insulted her. Papers were jammed, toner was everywhere, and somehow, the machine had printed an upside-down copy of the lunch menu from 1998. White, suppressing laughter, patted Mrs. Polk's shoulder and said, "You know, they say technology is supposed to make life easier. Clearly, they've never worked in a school." He then proceeded to do what all great leaders do—he called the one person who could fix everything: Ms. Patty, the secretary.

My First Lesson as a School Leader

Every wild thing has its rhyme and reason, and like the Wild Card in UNO, sometimes you've got to switch strategies on the fly to make it work.

This book aims to offer a different perspective. Mine. Lol. Seriously, take this walk with me to understand that what *really* happens when we accept the calling to be a school leader (in any capacity) is that we actually learn how our own personality contributes to our inability to make the connections needed to interact with others: teacher, students, parents, and whoever else may add to the success of teaching and learning for all involved.

In short, there's something "W.I.L.D." about each one of us! Ok, Dr. Vance. I'm not sure how I feel about being described as "wild". Take a look at these descriptions!

1. Wily & Innovative Leadership Dexterity–The ability to think on your feet, adapt, and problem-solve in unpredictable school situations

2. Whimsically Inspired Learning Disruptions–Those moments when students (or teachers) creatively push boundaries in ways that disrupt but also bring unexpected learning opportunities

3. Worn-out, Incapacitated, Laughably Delirious–The state of being an overworked school leader who finds the only way to survive is through strategic humor

Teaching Philosophy: Understanding the Wild Card

John Dewey's belief in experiential learning emphasizes that education must connect directly to the lived experiences of students. For WILD learners, this means creating environments where their unique ways of processing and interacting with the world are embraced rather than suppressed. Using strategies informed by Maslow's Hierarchy of Needs, addressing foundational needs—safety, belonging, and esteem—is critical for students and staff alike.

Creating environments that embrace WILD learners is critical because it fosters self-acceptance, maximizes potential, and allows them to develop skills necessary for lifelong success.

WILD individuals, including those with autism, ADHD, dyslexia, and other cognitive differences, often experience the world in ways that diverge from neurotypical norms. When their unique needs are met, they can thrive academically, socially, and professionally.

Why This Is Critical for Development?

1. Encourages Self-Confidence and Identity Formation

When WILD individuals feel valued, they develop self-confidence, leading to greater autonomy and self-advocacy.

2. Prevents Mental Health Challenges

Suppressing WILD traits can lead to anxiety, depression, and burnout. Environments that accept and adapt to their needs promote emotional well-being.

3. Enhances Learning and Skill Development

By leveraging strengths rather than focusing solely on deficits, WILD individuals can develop skills that align with their natural abilities.

4. Promotes Inclusion and Equity

Society benefits when diverse ways of thinking are integrated into education, workplaces, and communities. Different perspectives drive innovation and creativity.

WILD Tip:

Recognize sensory triggers for students and staff. Provide quiet spaces or alternative settings for those who may need them. Create sensory-friendly events to accommodate a wider range of participation. One of my favorite elementary schools in Mobile, AL uses "Zen Dens" for every grade. These rooms are open to all staff members who just need a break from the overstimulation that comes from attending to your own life, combined with the lives of others INCLUDING your students! Their school counselor continues to find ways to meet their hard work with zones that allow them to simply catch their breath.

What Could That Look Like, Globally?

Understanding Non-conformist Students in Educational Contexts

Non-conformist students challenge traditional learning structures, not out of defiance but from a need for autonomy, creativity, and meaningful engagement. Rather than viewing these students as disruptive, educators can embrace their unique perspectives and create environments where they can thrive.

Different countries approach the needs of WILD (Wonderfully Individualistic Learners with Divergence) students in unique ways, particularly in Finland and Japan, which have both made significant strides in inclusive and structured education while maintaining high standards.

How Finland Supports Non-conformist Students

Finland's educational system is known for its student-centered, flexible, and stigma-free approach, making it particularly effective in supporting students who push boundaries, think differently, or struggle with traditional academic expectations.

1. Collaborative Learning & Flexible Classroom Structures

How It Helps Nonconformists: Instead of enforcing rigid classroom norms, Finland embraces collaborative learning, where students work together to co-create knowledge.

Application: Instead of punishing a student who refuses to follow a specific assignment format, Finnish educators allow for student agency, providing various learning pathways.

Example: Non-conformist Student in Finland

Student: Mikko, a 10-year-old student, resists structured lesson plans and prefers open-ended discussions. In a traditional school, he might be labeled as "difficult."

Finnish Approach: Mikko's teacher allows him to participate in peer-driven discussions where students take turns leading class conversations. He thrives when given some control over the learning process.

2. Sensory-Sensitive Classrooms to Reduce Stigma Around Neurodiversity & WILD Behaviors

How It Helps Nonconformists: Many non-conformist students have unique sensory needs, whether it is because of neurodivergence (e.g., ADHD, Autism) or just personal learning preferences.

Application: Finnish schools often provide quiet spaces, sensory-friendly environments, and alternative seating arrangements (e.g., standing desks and fidget-friendly options).

Example: Sensory-Sensitive Support for a Nonconformist

Student: Ella, a student who dislikes sitting in one spot for long periods, often paces around the room or gets up mid-lesson. In traditional settings, she might be reprimanded for "not paying attention."

Finnish Approach: Instead of forcing her to sit, her teacher provides standing desks and flexible seating. Ella can move while learning, reducing behavioral disruptions while respecting her learning style.

How Japan Supports Non-conformist Students

Japan's education system is known for its discipline, structure, and high expectations, yet it has also developed strategies to accommodate diverse learners through mindfulness and precision-based instruction.

1. Incorporating Mindfulness for Self-Regulation

 How It Helps Nonconformists: Many non-conformist students are impulsive, energetic, or highly reactive when they feel constrained by rules.

 Application: Japanese schools integrate daily mindfulness exercises, including breathing techniques, meditation, and structured reflection periods, to help students develop emotional regulation.

Example: Non-conformist Student in Japan

Student: Taro, a high-energy student, frequently interrupts lessons with off-topic but intelligent questions. Rather than shutting him down, teachers use mindfulness techniques to help him self-regulate.

Japanese Approach: Before class discussions, Taro participates in a short meditation exercise to help focus his thoughts. Instead of feeling like an outsider, he learns self-awareness skills that allow him to take part meaningfully.

2. Precision-Based Instruction for Students Who Resist Generalized Learning

 How It Helps Nonconformists: Some non-conformist students dislike broad or abstract learning methods and prefer precision and mastery.

Application: Japanese schools emphasize precision-based learning, where students master one concept at a time before moving on, reducing frustration among students who demand structure in their learning process.

Example: Precision-Based Learning for a Nonconformist

Student: Hana, a detail-oriented student, dislikes broad essay prompts because she prefers concrete, step-by-step guidance. She struggles with vague assignments that require too much interpretation.

Japanese Approach: Instead of giving an open-ended essay, her teacher breaks down the process into smaller, logical steps—outlining, drafting, revising—allowing Hana to focus on mastering each phase without feeling overwhelmed.

Actionable Strategies for Supporting Non-conformist Students in Any Classroom

1. Build Relationships by Focusing on Everyone's Story (This is KEY!)

Why It Matters: Non-conformist students often feel misunderstood. Building meaningful teacher-student relationships helps them feel valued rather than isolated.

How to Do It:

- Have "Student Spotlight" Weeks, where each student shares

something unique about themselves.

- Conduct 1-on-1 check-ins to understand each student's learning style and motivation.

- Use interest-based learning, tailoring assignments to their passions.

Example: Relationship-Building with a Non-conformist Student

Student: Julian, a ninth grader, often refuses to write standard essays, claiming they are "pointless."

Teacher's Approach: Instead of forcing compliance, the teacher asks Julian about his interests (he loves music) and allows him to analyze song lyrics instead of a traditional literature assignment.

Result: Julian remains engaged while still developing critical analysis skills.

2. Host Collaborative Storytelling Workshops Where Students & Staff Share Perspectives

Why It Matters: Nonconformists thrive on open dialogue and discussion. Hosting collaborative storytelling sessions allows them to engage authentically while learning from others.

How to Do It:

- Organize "Teacher & Student Swap Stories" sessions, where both groups share personal learning experiences.

- Use peer-led storytelling, where students tell personal anecdotes and discuss different viewpoints.

- Assign perspective-shifting activities, where students argue both sides of an issue.

Example: Storytelling for a Non-conformist Student

Student: Naomi, an outspoken eighth grader, constantly challenges school rules, arguing for more student rights and freedoms.

Teacher's Approach: Instead of dismissing her concerns, her teacher hosts a mock town hall where students can propose and debate new school policies.

Result: Naomi learns how to advocate respectfully, and all students acquire civic engagement skills.

Chapter 2
The WILD Card Strategy

"Cause sometimes you gotta shuffle the whole deck just to keep folks guessing."

Let me tell you something real quick before we get all academic and strategic: if you have never had to problem-solve in heels, with a walkie in one hand, coffee in the other, and a third grader crying because their goldfish died *again*—baby, you haven't lived the full school leadership experience.

We do not talk about this enough, but some days, the job ain't in the handbook. It's in the hallway. More times than not, the plan you had at 7:00 a.m. gets hijacked by 8:03 because someone decided to bring their emotional support chicken to school... again.

Now listen—every school has a *WILD card*. You know the ones. The student who reenacts full Marvel fight scenes during math. The teacher who insists on glitter in every lesson (*and* lunch duty). The parent who sends four-paragraph emails with emojis *and* attachments... at 2:00 a.m.

Here's the thing: *WILD cards* aren't just chaos creators—they are culture shifters. They're unpredictable, yes—but also unforgettable. If you learn how to play your cards right, they become the heartbeat of your building.

Now, that's where strategy comes in. Not the kind you find in a binder collecting dust, but the kind that requires soul, wit, and a little gumbo seasoning. You've got to know when to redirect with humor, when to hug it out, and when to pull that mic and turn a pep rally disaster into a school legend. (Shout out to the unmasked mascot—who knew the shy kid had moves?)

This chapter is your invitation to step into the kind of leadership that *doesn't panic when the fire alarm goes off during lunch*, but instead says, "Welp… I guess we're having recess with snacks today."

The WILD card strategy is all about knowing your people, reading the room, and leading with enough grace and grit to laugh when the macaroni masterpiece goes missing—again.

Sometimes leadership is not about the perfect plan. It's about the perfect pivot! Let's look at a few scenarios!

The Pep Rally Pandemonium

Principal Anderson was hyped for the big school pep rally. Everything was going according to plan—until the mascot's head fell off mid-dance routine, revealing the shyest, most unsuspecting eighth grader in history. The gym fell silent. For a moment, time stood still. Then, from the bleachers, a lone voice shouted, "The mascot is one of us!" Just like that, the student body erupted into a standing ovation.

Thinking quickly, Anderson grabbed the mic and announced, "And that, my friends, is the true spirit of our school—every student, a hero in disguise!" The crowd went wild, and the eighth grader became an overnight legend.

The Great Fire Drill Fake-Out

Assistant Principal Thomas took pride in being ultra-prepared for anything... except for a surprise fire drill—pulled by none other than the school's own overzealous technology teacher, who "accidentally" hit the wrong button while testing the PA system. As students streamed out of classrooms in what can only be described as organized chaos, Thomas spotted fourth-grader Benny walking *leisurely* while eating a fruit roll-up.

"Benny, it's a fire drill! You need to move faster!" Thomas called.

Without missing a beat, Benny replied, "Mr. Thomas, I don't *run* for fake fires."

The PTA Potluck Showdown

Veteran Principal Ms. Hernandez had survived many things—budget cuts, teacher shortages, even a surprise district visit on pajama day. Yet, nothing compared to the annual PTA potluck, where two rival parents waged a silent war over whose lasagna was superior.

This year, it reached peak absurdity when Mrs. Thompson *subtly* mentioned that her grandmother's "authentic Italian recipe" had won an award. Not to be outdone, Mrs. Martinez *accidentally* placed a printed-out Yelp review of her family's restaurant next to her tray.

Sensing imminent disaster, Hernandez grabbed a microphone and declared, "Well, it looks like we have a tie! I guess the only fair way to settle this is... a faculty vs. PTA lasagna cook-off next month!" The room cheered, and the rivalry was postponed (for now).

The Great Kindergarten Art Heist

Ms. Holloway, the energetic new principal, had just finished hanging student artwork when a tiny but serious-faced kindergartener approached her office.

"I need to report a crime," he said solemnly.

Concerned, Holloway leaned in. "Oh dear! What happened?"

The boy crossed his arms. "Somebody STOLE my macaroni masterpiece from the hallway."

Ms. Holloway, knowing the likelihood of *accidental macaroni redistribution* was high, walked him back to the display wall. Sure enough, another student's name was now written under the (admittedly identical) pasta creation.

Holloway thought fast. "You know, true artists inspire others. Maybe this means you're such a good artist that people want to claim your work!"

The boy narrowed his eyes, considering this. "Like Van Gogh?"

"EXACTLY like Van Gogh."

Satisfied, the student walked away, newfound confidence in tow.

The Mystery of the Missing Substitute

Mr. Patel, the assistant principal, was covering for a missing substitute teacher in a first-grade classroom when he noticed something... odd. The students kept looking at an empty chair and whispering.

Finally, one brave soul raised her hand. "Mr. Patel, the sub *is* here."

Patel looked around. "Where?"

A chorus of tiny voices answered: "She's invisible today."

Realizing the kids had *completely* convinced themselves of this imaginary teacher, Patel decided to roll with it. "Well then," he said, pulling out a notepad, "let's write a report for the principal about what she *taught* us today."

By the end of the day, Patel had a collection of the wildest, most creative "lessons" ever imagined—including a brand-new way to count using only pink crayons.

The WILD card in any card game is a game-changer. It can be anything you need—a lifeline, a way out, or a new beginning. As a school leader, being a WILD card means staying adaptable, knowing your team, and being ready to pivot when plans (inevitably) fall apart.

Strategies for Playing the WILD Card

1. Color Change–Adjust your approach to match the person or group you are working with. Howard Gardner's Multiple Intelligences theory highlights the diverse ways individuals process information. For WILD learners, focus on their specific strengths (visual-spatial, linguistic, logical-mathematical, etc.).

WILD Tip:

Recognize that flexibility in teaching methods benefits all learners. Incorporate visual aids, movement, and storytelling to engage students who may struggle with traditional teaching methods.

2. Draw Four–Vygotsky's Zone of Proximal Development suggests that tasks slightly beyond an individual's current ability, when scaffolded, can lead to significant growth. This applies equally to WILD students and overwhelmed teachers.

Strategies for Support Across the Lifespan

Infancy & Early Childhood (0-5 Years)

- Early Diagnosis & Intervention: Identify developmental differences early through screenings and assessments.

- Sensory-Friendly Environments: Provide safe spaces with appropriate lighting, textures, and noise levels.

- Play-Based Learning: Encourage exploration through hands-on, interactive play tailored to individual needs.

- Parent & Caregiver Training: Educate families on how to support communication, social engagement, and sensory processing differences.

School-Age (6-18 Years)

- Individualized Education Plans (IEPs) & 504 Plans: Develop personalized learning accommodations, such as extended time on tests, alternative communication methods, and movement breaks.

- Flexible Instructional Methods: Use multimodal teaching (visual, auditory, kinesthetic) to cater to different learning styles.

- Social Skills Support: Implement peer mentoring, structured social activities, and special interest clubs to build friendships.

- WILD-Affirming Discipline: Use restorative justice approaches rather than punitive measures that misunderstand behavioral expressions.

Higher Education & Early Adulthood (18-30 Years)

- College & Vocational Training Accommodations: Provide note-taking support, extended deadlines, and quiet study areas.

- Career Readiness Programs: Offer mentorship, job coaching, and strengths-based career matching.

- Independent Living Skills Training: Teach executive functioning strategies like time management, budgeting, and transportation planning.

- Mental Health Support: Ensure access to counselors who understand WILD and provide affirming care.

Adulthood (30-65 Years)

- Workplace Accommodations: Advocate for flexible work schedules, sensory-friendly office spaces, and assistive technology.

- WILD Leadership Initiatives: Create pathways for career advancement that value diverse cognitive approaches.

- Community Inclusion: Foster support networks through advocacy groups, professional organizations, and inclusive recreational activities.

- Health & Wellness Access: Ensure medical professionals are trained in WILD communication and care needs.

Late Adulthood & Aging (65+ Years)

- Support for Cognitive Changes: Recognize that WILD may intersect with aging-related conditions and adapt caregiving accordingly.

- Accessible Senior Living Options: Design environments that respect sensory sensitivities and routine-based needs.

- Lifelong Learning Opportunities: Provide continued education and engagement in hobbies that cater to WILD ways of thinking.

- Preserving Dignity & Advocacy: Encourage autonomy and decision-making in aging WILD individuals.

Supporting WILD individuals from birth to late adulthood requires a holistic, lifelong approach that respects their unique ways of experiencing the world. When society shifts from suppression to acceptance, WILD individuals can contribute their talents fully, leading to more inclusive communities where everyone thrives.

Here's the thing: embracing WILD personalities does not mean we abandon structure or expectations. It means we rethink how we define success. Instead of asking, "How do I get this kid to follow the rules?", we ask, "How do I guide this kid to lead with purpose?"

Now that, my friend, is where the growth mindset comes in. Because when we shift our lens from control to curiosity—from compliance to creativity—we unlock the real magic of education. We stop seeing kids as behavior problems and start seeing them as *potential* in progress.

A growth mindset is not just an idea—it is a way of showing up for our WILD learners. It's the belief that everyone, no matter how loud, squiggly, curious, or chaos-producing they are, can grow with the right support.

So, as we shuffle the deck and play our WILD cards with heart and humor, let's also deal in some belief—that every wild thing can grow wiser, stronger, and more fully themselves with time, trust, and a little bit of guided mischief.

Real-World Examples & Strategies for Implementing Growth Mindset + Curiosity in Education

To truly embed a growth mindset and curiosity-driven learning into a school's culture, educational leaders must model, encourage, and sustain these approaches through strategic professional development and classroom implementation. Below are real-world examples and actionable strategies at different levels:

1. Professional Development for Educators: Growth Mindset in Action

Example: The "Failure Showcase" Initiative (I've created a sample PD you can find in the Appendices.)

A middle school principal wanted teachers to embrace a growth mindset and normalize failure as part of learning. Instead of a traditional professional development meeting, she hosted a "Failure Showcase," where teachers shared personal classroom failures and what they learned from them.

Outcome: Teachers saw failures as stepping stones rather than setbacks, making them more open to trying new teaching strategies without fear. They also modeled vulnerability for students, reinforcing that learning is a process.

How to Implement:

- Host quarterly "Failure to Flourish" teacher reflections where educators share what did not work and brainstorm solutions together.

- Encourage admin-led growth mindset coaching—principals should model risk-taking and adaptability in their leadership.

- Provide growth-focused feedback instead of solely evaluating performance. Focus on improvement, not just outcomes.

2. Encouraging Curiosity-Driven Learning in the Classroom

Example: The "Wonder Wall" Strategy

A high school science teacher found that students often hesitated to ask questions for fear of sounding "dumb." She created a "Wonder Wall" where students anonymously posted any question they had about science—even if it seemed unrelated to the current unit.

Outcome: The teacher used these questions to guide inquiry-based lessons, letting students explore answers themselves. Over time, students became more engaged and confident in asking questions out loud.

How to Implement:

- Create a physical or digital Wonder Wall where students can write down questions anonymously. Dedicate class time to exploring them.

- Use mystery-driven lessons (e.g., "Why do some animals glow?" or "How do we know the Earth isn't flat?") to spark curiosity.

- Challenge students with Socratic Sessions where they discuss open-ended, complex questions.

3. School-Wide Culture Shift: Fostering Curiosity & Growth

Example: "Curiosity Challenges" in Morning Announcements

A K-8 school introduced weekly curiosity challenges where students were given a question or problem to solve (e.g., "How could we redesign our playground to be more accessible?" or "Why do seasons change?"). Students worked in teams and presented creative solutions during Friday assemblies.

Outcome:

- There was increased collaboration and problem-solving among students.

- Students developed intrinsic motivation—they wanted to find answers not just for grades but for fun.

- Teachers reported a shift in student engagement—kids asked deeper questions and made connections beyond their curriculum.

How to Implement:

- Incorporate daily or weekly curiosity prompts in morning meetings or school newsletters.

- Have teachers start lessons with "What if?" or "Why does this matter?" instead of just presenting facts.

- Allow students to design their own learning projects around topics they find interesting.

4. Growth Mindset & Curiosity in Assessments

Example: The "Rework & Reflect" Grading System

An elementary school removed traditional letter grades for formative assessments and instead adopted a Rework & Reflect model. Instead of receiving a failing grade, students got feedback and were required to revise their work and explain what they learned from their mistakes.

Outcome:

- Students stopped fearing mistakes and began seeing failure as a natural part of learning.

- Instead of feeling discouraged, they gained confidence in their ability to improve over time.

- Teachers spent less time justifying bad grades and more time guiding students toward mastery.

How to Implement:

- Allow students to revise assessments & assignments with teacher guidance.

- Use growth-based report cards that include feedback on effort and resilience, not just test scores.

- Encourage self-reflection journals where students track how they overcame challenges in learning.

5. Leadership & Staff Engagement: Modeling Growth & Curiosity

Example: The "Try Something New" Challenge for Staff

A district superintendent challenged all staff members—from teachers to custodians—to learn a new skill or try a new approach for one month. At the end of the month, they shared their experiences at a faculty meeting.

Outcome:

- Staff developed empathy for students who struggle with new concepts.

- It reinforced a culture of lifelong learning among educators.

- It created cross-department collaboration, as people learned from one another's experiences.

How to Implement:

- Start faculty meetings with a quick "What I Tried" reflection where staff share one new method they experimented with in the classroom.

- Encourage cross-grade collaboration, where high school and elementary teachers share different perspectives on learning.

- Develop staff book clubs around growth mindset and curiosity-driven learning (e.g., *Mindset* by Carol Dweck, *Make It Stick* by Peter C. Brown).

Growth Mindset + Curiosity = Transformational Learning

When students, teachers, and school leaders embrace challenges as opportunities and lean into curiosity as a driver of learning, schools become places of inspiration, resilience, and innovation.

By embedding these practices into daily instruction, school culture, assessments, and leadership, we move beyond just teaching content—we cultivate lifelong learners and problem solvers who aren't afraid to take on the unknown.

Educating and Guiding Non-conforming Students: A Global Perspective on Adaptability

Non-conforming students—those who challenge norms, question authority, and learn in unconventional ways—are often misunderstood in traditional school systems. Yet, when given the right support, they can become some of the most innovative thinkers, problem solvers, and change makers in society. Across the globe, different educational systems have found creative ways to adapt to the needs of diverse learners, proving that adaptability, rather than conformity, is the key to unlocking student potential.

Global Perspectives on Adaptability

Rural Schools in Sub-Saharan Africa: Innovation Through Resourcefulness

In rural areas of Sub-Saharan Africa, adaptability isn't a luxury—it's a necessity. Schools often operate with limited resources, but this scarcity fosters creativity. Teachers don't always have access to the latest educational tools, so they turn to local materials, oral storytelling traditions, and community knowledge to make learning relevant and engaging.

Lessons for Supporting Non-conforming Students:

- Emphasizing real-world learning: Instead of rigid, standardized curriculums, students learn through hands-on activities like agricultural projects, business simulations, and apprenticeship-style learning.

- Cultural inclusion: Instead of forcing students into a one-size-fits-all education model, teachers weave local customs, histories, and experiences into lessons, making learning feel personal and meaningful.

- Student-driven problem solving: Many schools encourage students to find their own solutions to challenges, fostering critical thinking and leadership skills—perfect for non-conforming minds that thrive on independence.

Urban Schools in North America: Leveraging Technology for Individualized Learning

In contrast, urban schools in North America face a different challenge: how to keep up with the fast-paced, technology-driven world that constantly shifts and changes. Here, adaptability means using technology to engage diverse learners, including those who resist traditional classroom structures.

Lessons for Supporting Non-conforming Students:

- Personalized learning paths: Non-conforming students often struggle in rigid learning environments. Schools use AI-driven platforms and online learning tools to allow students to work at their own pace and explore topics that interest them.

- Gamification & interactive learning: Some students reject traditional assignments but excel when engaged through educational games, coding challenges, and virtual simulations that feel more immersive and interactive.

- Alternative assessment methods: Instead of relying solely on standardized tests, teachers assess students through portfolio projects, video presentations, and digital storytelling, allowing non-conforming learners to showcase their strengths in unique ways.

Actionable Strategies to Support Non-conforming Students

1. Use Peer Mentors for WILD Students to Model Social and Academic Behaviors

Non-conforming students often resist authority figures but respond well to peer influence. Implementing peer mentorship programs can help these students develop essential social and academic skills in a way that feels natural and less imposed.

What this looks like in practice:

- Pair non-conforming students with older or more experienced peers who have successfully navigated the school system without losing their individuality.

- Introduce "reverse mentoring", where WILD students teach peers and even teachers something they excel at (e.g., technology skills, creative problem-solving).

- Allow peer mentors to act as academic guides—helping non-conforming students break large tasks into manageable steps while reinforcing the value of persistence and effort.

Why this works:

- Encourages social-emotional learning in a way that feels authentic.

- Reduces feelings of isolation that many non-conforming students experience.

- Promotes self-advocacy—students see that they don't have to "fit in" to succeed, they just need the right strategies.

2. Provide Incremental Professional Development for Staff

Too often, professional development (PD) for educators is delivered in one-size-fits-all training sessions that don't address the complexity of supporting non-conforming students. Instead, schools should provide incremental, hands-on training that builds educators' capacity to meet the needs of WILD learners over time.

What this looks like in practice:

- Micro-PD sessions that focus on small, implementable strategies rather than overwhelming teachers with an entire philosophy at once.

- On-the-job coaching where specialists work directly with teachers in the classroom to model and refine approaches for engaging non-conforming students.

- Teacher learning communities where educators share successes and troubleshoot challenges together, ensuring continuous adaptation.

Why this works:

- Breaks down resistance to change by introducing new strategies in manageable steps.

- Fosters collaboration between general education and special education teachers, making sure all students receive the support they need.

- Encourages teachers to embrace adaptability—instead of expecting students to fit into the system, they learn to adjust the system to fit students.

Guiding the Wild Toward Wisdom

Non-conforming students, like the world around them, are unpredictable, imaginative, and full of untapped potential. Instead of forcing them into rigid structures, educators and community leaders must create environments where wildness is not only accepted but encouraged as a driver of innovation.

The global examples from Sub-Saharan Africa and North America remind us that adaptability isn't about lowering standards—it's about expanding possibilities. By using peer mentorship and incremental professional development, we can create a school culture where WILD students don't feel like outsiders—they feel like PIONEERS. Remember Max and Scott from the Forward examples? Today's nonconformists are tomorrow's visionaries—our job isn't to tame them. It's to help them navigate their wildness toward wisdom, growth, and success.

How Teachers Can Support Non-conformist Students

Nonconformists don't have to be a challenge in the classroom—they can be some of the most creative, engaged, and exciting students to teach if given the right environment.

1. Give Them a Voice & Choice

- Instead of forcing compliance, find ways to let them take ownership of their learning.

- Offer multiple options for assignments (e.g., essay, presentation, video, art project).

- Allow student-led discussions where they can challenge ideas and think critically.

- Encourage self-directed learning, where they explore topics they care about.

Funny Anecdote: A teacher once told a student they could present their research project "in any format." The student showed up in a full suit, gave a TED Talk-style speech, and took audience questions. *Challenge accepted!*

2. Acknowledge Their Perspective (Even When You Disagree)!

- Instead of shutting down their challenges, engage in dialogue with them.

- If they challenge a classroom rule, explain the reasoning behind it.

- If they bring up a different opinion, ask them to back it up with evidence.

- Let them know that questioning things is okay, but it should be done respectfully and constructively.

A middle schooler refused to do a history assignment on George Washington because "he didn't actually have wooden teeth, and this is revisionist history!" The teacher laughed and let the student research and write a *fact-checking* version of the assignment instead.

3. Use Humor & Playfulness to Diffuse Resistance

- If a student is resisting for the sake of pushing boundaries, sometimes humor is the best response.

- If a student challenges a rule, say, *"Okay, convince me why you should be allowed to wear a cape to class."*

- If they push back on an assignment, jokingly say, *"You want to write your book report in the form of a rap battle? I'm listening."*

A student argued that school should start at noon. The teacher made them write a persuasive letter to the principal, using research. The student later admitted, *"Okay, fine, but can we at least start at 9:30?"*

4. Set Clear Boundaries Without Stifling Creativity

Nonconformity is great, but structure is still important. Let them push the envelope *within* a safe framework.

- Set non-negotiables (e.g., "We debate ideas, but we respect each other").

- Allow freedom *within* guidelines (e.g., "You can express yourself in your writing, but it must be school-appropriate").

- Encourage constructive rebellion (e.g., "If you want to change a rule, create a solid argument for it").

5. Tap into Their Strengths

Instead of seeing nonconformity as a problem, find ways to channel it productively.

- Let them lead a classroom debate.

- Allow them to explore passion projects.

- Encourage creative thinking in assignments.

Chapter 3

Taming the Wild Child (And Their Wild Teacher) While Fostering their Unique Gifts

C onsider the time Ms. Mensah, a wildly creative third grade teacher from Ghana, decided her classroom theme for the year was "Jungle of Genius." She turned her *entire* room into a rainforest. Paper vines hung from the ceiling, native animal sounds played in the background, and she wore a safari hat every Monday.

She had the kids so excited about learning that even Amir, our usually unbothered student who treated school like a part-time gig, came in roaring like a lion during spelling tests.

Of course, not everyone was amused. Mr. Vaughn, a more traditional 5th grade teacher, peeked into her class one morning and muttered, "It looks like Animal Planet exploded in here."

Still, test scores soared.

Kids started calling their mistakes "jungle jumps"—opportunities to swing to the next level.

Wild? Yes. Effective? Absolutely. Ms. Mensah turned curiosity into culture, and chaos into creativity.

Then there was Coach Parkinson, who once taught a lesson on gravity by launching watermelons off the school roof (don't ask about the insurance paperwork). The kids? Engaged. The watermelon? R.I.P. The lesson? Unforgettable.

Plus, who could forget when young Kareem, a spirited kindergartener from Detroit, convinced his entire class that his imaginary pet lizard Larry was the class mascot? By Friday, even the janitor was leaving snacks for Larry in the corner.

Oh, and don't let me leave out Kyla from D.C., who once brought her pet guinea pig dressed as Harriet Tubman for Black History Month and gave a full speech on why courage comes in all sizes. Ma'am—pass the mic.

The 7-Year-Old Philosopher

"Why do we even have school if we can just Google everything?" Jiana asked me one morning. The teacher had sent her to the office for being "disruptive," but the gleam in her eye told me this kid was just wildly curious.

Teaching Philosophy: Curiosity as a Catalyst

Carol Dweck's growth mindset highlights the importance of seeing challenges as opportunities to develop new skills. For WILD learners like

Jiana, this means providing outlets for their curiosity in structured ways that benefit their academic journey.

Curiosity is the foundation of a thriving learning environment. When students are encouraged to ask questions, explore ideas, and investigate new concepts, they develop intrinsic motivation—the drive to learn for the sake of learning.

This teaching philosophy aligns perfectly with the growth mindset as it encourages students to see challenges as invitations to discover new knowledge rather than obstacles to avoid.

Why Curiosity-Driven Learning Matters:

1. Engagement Over Compliance – Students retain more information when they are genuinely interested, rather than just completing assignments for a grade.

2. Problem-Solving & Critical Thinking – When students learn to ask "Why?" and "How?", they develop essential analytical and problem-solving skills.

3. Confidence in Learning – A classroom that values curiosity fosters intellectual bravery, where students take risks without fear of failure.

How Educators Can Use Curiosity as a Catalyst

- Encourage Inquiry-Based Learning – Instead of simply providing answers, teachers can pose open-ended questions that challenge students to think critically.

- Use Real-World Problems – Connect lessons to authentic, real-world issues that make learning meaningful and relevant.

- Foster a "What If?" Classroom Culture – Encourage students to explore possibilities by asking "What if we tried this another way?" or "How else could we solve this?"

- Normalize "Not Knowing" – Teachers and leaders should model intellectual humility, showing that it's okay not to have all the answers, as long as you're willing to find them.

Bringing It All Together: Growth Mindset + Curiosity in Action

When educators embrace both a growth mindset and curiosity-driven teaching, they create a learning environment where students:

- View failure as feedback rather than defeat.

- Seek out challenges instead of avoiding them.

- Develop resilience and grit by persisting through difficulties.

- Become lifelong learners who find joy in discovering new ideas.

By seeing challenges as opportunities and using curiosity as a catalyst, we build not just stronger students—but independent thinkers, creative problem-solvers, and adaptable future leaders.

Examples Across Borders

India

Curiosity-driven learning is integrated into schools using hands-on experiments, even in resource-limited environments.

Australia

Creativity in learning is celebrated with programs that integrate arts, fostering engagement for WILD students.

Actionable Strategies:

1. Create Genius Hour sessions where students can explore their own questions.

2. Design reward systems that honor effort over outcomes.

Chapter 4

Parents Are Wild Cards, Too

Parents Are Wild Cards, Too: Navigating Rebellious Learners Through Strong Partnerships

Now, parents, they are the ultimate mystery cards! Some come with a manual, some come with fireworks. Either way, they're part of the team.

Picture it—Parent-Teacher Night.

We had one parent, Mrs. Hernandez, who brought a full binder of color-coded tabs labeled: "Concerns," "Compliments," and "Conspiracy Theories." She grilled us about curriculum standards, cell tower radiation, and whether school pizza had real cheese. Bless her heart.

Then there was Mr. Zhao, who came in with his son, Lee, holding a drone. He said, "Lee wants to show you his social studies project." That child re-created the Boston Tea Party—with drones, LEGOs, and a real-time commentary in three languages. It took out half the bulletin board, but it was magnificent.

And then there's Ms. Jackson, a grandmother from Alabama raising her twin grandbabies. She walked into the IEP meeting wearing a full church hat and holding a folder that said "Try Me." She was kind, firm, and full of wisdom—and had the best one-liners like, "My babies might be spicy, but they ain't rotten."

Let's not forget Mr. Singh, who once asked if his son Arjun could "opt out of homework to pursue higher enlightenment." We compromised with a science fair project on meditative brainwaves. Wild? Yup. Enlightening? Also, yes.

> Every parent has their own brand of wild—and guess what? That wildness is often a mirror of their child's brilliance. The key isn't taming it. It's listening, laughing a little, and learning from it. Because a parent who shows up—be it with drones or dairy-free pizza complaints—is still showing up.

When working with WILD students—those who challenge the traditional learning mold with their rebellious, creative, or unconventional approaches—it's easy to forget that their behaviors don't exist in isolation. They are shaped by their home environments, experiences, and, most importantly, the ultimate wildcard factor: their parents.

Some parents arrive ready to collaborate, armed with data, research, and color-coded binders. Others show up questioning every assignment, every consequence, and whether school is even necessary at all. Some are disengaged. Some are over-involved, and some...well, some might just email you at 2:00 AM about a missing worksheet.

Regardless of where they land on the spectrum, parents of WILD students are key players in shaping their child's educational journey, and building partnerships with them is essential.

The challenge? Figuring out how to work with parents who may also have their own rebellious approach to the system.

Building Parent Partnerships with Epstein's Six Types of Involvement

Joyce Epstein's Framework of Six Types of Involvement provides a roadmap for schools to engage families in ways that benefit both the student and the learning environment. Applying this framework to WILD students and their equally unpredictable parents allows educators to create meaningful connections that turn resistance into collaboration.

Parenting: Understanding Their Child's Needs

The Reality:

Some parents of WILD students see their child's rebellion as independence. Others feel overwhelmed or unsure how to provide support. Some have had negative experiences with the school system themselves and are skeptical of authority.

How to Approach It:

- Shift the narrative. Instead of framing the student as "difficult," frame them as a unique thinker who needs tailored support.

- Offer parenting workshops on topics like growth mindset, executive functioning skills, and social-emotional learning.

- Provide strength-based profiles of students that highlight their natural leadership, creativity, or problem-solving skills alongside areas needing growth.

Example: A parent who refuses to enforce homework time at home may not be "ignoring school," but rather prioritizing family connection. Finding a middle ground—like project-based assignments that encourage family involvement—might make them more likely to engage.

Communicating: Creating Open and Honest Conversations

The Reality:

Not all parents want weekly emails, or a behavior report every time their kid refuses to write an essay in cursive "because it's a dead language." Some thrive on in-person check-ins, while others would rather text than talk.

How to Approach It:

- Meet them where they are. If a parent responds best via text, use text. If they need a face-to-face, set up meetings around their availability.

- Use humor and authenticity. Many parents of WILD students already know their kid is a challenge—they don't need another lecture.

- Create two-way communication by asking, "What's working at home?" instead of just reporting what's going wrong at school.

Example: Instead of sending a formal "Johnny refused to participate" note, try: *"Hey, Johnny had some big opinions about today's lesson on poetry. Any chance he'd be open to writing a rap version instead? Let me know what you think!"*

Volunteering: Finding Their Strengths

The Reality:

Some parents want to be involved in school but don't feel comfortable in traditional volunteer roles. Others would rather coach a robot-building team than bake cookies for the PTA.

How to Approach It:

- Ask "What are your skills?" instead of "Can you chaperone?" A parent who is a mechanic might love to run a hands-on STEM workshop. A parent who's an artist might enjoy helping create a mural.

- Create non-traditional volunteer opportunities—like "Help from Home" projects where parents can contribute without stepping inside the school.

- Involve parents in their child's passion areas. If a WILD student loves music, invite their parents to a music-related event instead of a general meeting.

Example: A parent who never attended a parent-teacher conference shows up for Career Day when they can talk about their job as a music producer.

Learning at Home: Connecting School to Real Life

The Reality:

Many WILD students thrive in hands-on, real-world learning but struggle with worksheets, rote memorization, or "because I said so" explanations. Parents might feel frustrated with school assignments that seem disconnected from life.

How to Approach It:

- Make homework meaningful. Instead of 20 math problems, give a real-world budgeting challenge.

- Provide family learning experiences, like interactive projects where students interview parents or create presentations on family traditions.

- Offer alternative assignments for parents who actively reject traditional education models.

Example: Instead of a "write about a historical event" assignment, a student with a mechanic parent might build a model of the first car engine and explain its evolution.

Decision-Making: Giving Parents a Voice

The Reality:

Some parents feel disempowered by the school system and believe their concerns aren't valued. Others want a say but don't feel comfortable in formal PTA meetings.

How to Approach It:

- Invite parents to serve on committees that directly impact their child's education, such as curriculum advisory boards or discipline policy reviews.

- Offer casual, low-pressure meetings, like Coffee with the Principal, where parents can share ideas informally.

- Acknowledge their expertise. Parents are their child's first teacher—ask them for input and act on it.

Example: A parent who criticizes school discipline policies is invited to co-develop a positive behavior initiative, turning criticism into contribution.

Collaborating with the Community: Expanding Resources

The Reality:

Not all parents have the time, energy, or resources to fully engage in school activities, but many want to contribute in ways that matter.

How to Approach It:

- Partner with local businesses and organizations that align with student interests (e.g., makerspaces for hands-on learners, coding workshops for tech-savvy students).

- Connect parents with external support services for mental health, financial aid, or tutoring.

- Recognize that "involvement" looks different for every family—celebrate engagement in all its forms.

Example: A school partners with a local skate shop to sponsor a physics-in-skateboarding workshop, bringing in students *and* parents who might otherwise disengage.

Final Thoughts: Wild Kids, Wild Parents, and Wild Wins

Just like their kids, parents can be rule-followers, challengers, skeptics, or trailblazers. The goal isn't to force them into a box but to find ways to connect that honor their strengths.

When schools shift from seeing parents as obstacles to seeing them as assets, the entire learning experience transforms. Wild students become empowered learners, wild parents become engaged partners, and educators stop feeling like they're fighting a battle alone.

So, the next time you meet a wild parent, remember: Every wild card can be played to your advantage—if you learn how to use it.

.

How Parents Can Support Non-conformist Children

1. Encourage Their Individuality (While Teaching Social Skills)

Nonconformity should be embraced, but kids still need to learn how to function in society.

- Encourage their unique interests and passions.

- Teach them how to challenge ideas respectfully.

- Help them learn when to pick their battles.

2. Advocate for Them in School

Work with teachers to ensure your child is being supported, not disciplined unfairly.

- If they struggle with traditional assignments, ask about alternative learning options.

- Encourage open dialogue with teachers about how they learn best.

3. Expose Them to Role Models Who Were Nonconformists

Show them how successful people challenged norms but still worked within society.

- Introduce them to inventors, artists, and activists who pushed boundaries.

- Read about entrepreneurs like Steve Jobs or scientists like Albert Einstein.

Global Practices

Latin America

Schools foster partnerships by hosting family learning nights where parents and children learn together.

Europe

Collaborative decision-making between parents and educators ensures WILD needs are met.

Actionable Strategies:

1. Host WILD awareness nights to educate families.

2. Provide clear, jargon-free communication about Individualized Education Programs (IEPs).

Chapter 5

The Power of Humor in Leadership

School leadership is NOT for the faint of heart. If you can laugh—at yourself, with others, and occasionally at the absurdity of it all—you'll survive.

When I first became an administrator, I thought leadership was all polished blazers and district-approved talking points. Well, let me tell you—true leadership is keeping a straight face while a second grader explains how he cannot possibly do math today because Mercury is in retrograde.

Take Ms. Al-Saleh, our counselor from Dearborn. She used to hold "Feelings Friday" in the cafeteria with a giant plush emoji pillow. Kids could tap it to say how they were feeling. One day, a student named DeShawn threw it in the trash and yelled, "Today, I feel TRASHED!"

Did we panic? Nope. Ms. Al-Saleh calmly pulled it out, dusted it off, and said, "Well, at least you're honest, baby." Everyone cracked up. Humor diffused the moment, and we still got to talk about emotional regulation.

Laughter is how we build bridges—with kids, with staff, with our sanity.

And I'll never forget when Principal Dlamini from South Africa visited our school and asked during dismissal chaos, "Is this the apocalypse or just Thursday?" We laughed for days.

And how could I not mention when a kindergartener handed me a sticky note with the words: "You are not the boss of me, but I like your shoes." Flattery will get you far, baby.

> Humor is more than just a stress reliever; it's a **bridge** that connects students, parents, and staff in ways that traditional leadership strategies often fail to do.

Ken Robinson's work on creativity reminds us that humor is often the gateway to innovative thinking, problem-solving, and authentic engagement—especially for WILD learners, whose rebellious nature often thrives in unconventional spaces.

Humor as a Bridge for WILD Students

WILD learners—those who challenge norms, question authority, and resist rigid instruction—often struggle in traditional academic settings. But humor lowers defenses, builds trust, and makes learning feel less like a battle and more like an adventure.

The Science Behind Humor & Learning

- Laughter reduces stress and anxiety, helping students feel safe enough to engage.

- Humor increases dopamine production, which enhances motivation and memory retention.

- When students see teachers and leaders as relatable, they are more likely to buy into the learning process.

Example: A high school history teacher once started his lesson on revolutions by walking into class wearing a powdered wig and declaring, "I AM GEORGE WASHINGTON. ASK ME ANYTHING." The students laughed—but then engaged in an impromptu, high-energy discussion about leadership, war, and historical perspectives. The humor broke down resistance and sparked curiosity.

Wild Strategy: Instead of disciplining WILD students for being class clowns, redirect their energy into creative projects, like having them write their own satirical take on a lesson or lead a debate in the voice of a historical figure.

Using Humor to Build Social Connections

For WILD students—many of whom struggle with social norms, anxiety, or authority figures—humor can serve as a bridge to connection.

Ways Humor Builds Social Connection:

- Encourages collaborative storytelling, where students co-create jokes or comedic skits about a lesson.

- Helps neurodiverse students feel more socially included in ways that don't pressure them into forced interactions.

- Reinforces teacher-student bonds, helping educators be seen as approachable, rather than adversarial.

Example: A principal dealing with a defiant middle schooler who refused to participate in class handed her a "Most Likely to Argue with a Rock" award. The student laughed, and from that moment on, they engaged in class debates instead of shutting down.

Humor flipped resistance into participation.

Wild Strategy: Let WILD students write class superlatives—not just for each other, but for school subjects. Imagine a math class where students label Algebra as "Most Likely to Make Me Cry" or English as "Most Likely to Inspire My Future TED Talk."

Humor & Leadership: Laugh or Cry, You Choose

Being a school leader means balancing crises, complaints, and complete unpredictability—often within the span of a single morning.

The best leaders know that humor isn't just a survival tool—it's a leadership strategy.

How Leaders Use Humor to Manage Chaos:

- De-escalation Tool: Light humor can diffuse tense parent-teacher conferences, redirect power struggles, and ease anxiety in difficult conversations.

- Team Morale Booster: A <u>well-timed</u> joke can reset a staff meeting, relieve stress, and make administrators seem more human.

- Resilience Builder: When school leaders laugh at themselves, they model emotional intelligence and adaptability for staff and students.

Example: A superintendent walking into a chaotic cafeteria, surveying the scene of spilled juice, overturned chairs, and a group of students dramatically arguing about TikTok, sighs and says, "So THIS is why we can't have nice things." The tension breaks. Staff laughs. The problem still needs solving, but now, everyone is approaching it with less stress and more perspective.

Wild Strategy: Create a "School Leadership Blooper Reel" tradition—a staff-led storytelling session where teachers and admins share their funniest "oops" moments from the school year. Bonus points are rewarded if they involve mispronounced student names, technology malfunctions, or PTA meeting mishaps.

The Wild Card Leader's Guide to Using Humor Effectively

NOT LAME:

- Use humor to relate, not to belittle. (Laugh WITH, not AT.)

- Keep it situational, tied to real classroom or leadership experiences.

- Adapt it to different students—some love sarcasm, others need gentle humor.

- Be self-deprecating when appropriate—it makes you more relatable.

LAME:

- Use humor to dismiss student concerns (e.g., "Oh, you think THAT assignment is hard? Try paying taxes!")

- Make jokes at a student's expense—they should always feel safe.

- Use humor as a cop-out to avoid difficult conversations.

If You Can Laugh, You Can Lead!

Leadership is hard, but humor makes it lighter. For WILD students, humor isn't just about entertainment—it's a tool for learning, connection, and self-expression.

The next time your day goes completely off the rails—when the Wi-Fi crashes during testing, a kindergarten class accidentally sets off the fire alarm, or a parent emails you at 2:00 AM about a missing permission slip from three months ago—remember:

The fact of the matter is this: You can cry, or you can laugh. And laughing is way more fun to ME!

International Applications

Brazil

Dialogic teaching (using ongoing dialogue between teacher and student) is integral to many classrooms, fostering an environment of mutual respect and understanding.

Scandinavia

Student-led conferences encourage ownership of learning and advocacy.

Actionable Strategies:

1. Incorporate improv games into professional development.

2. Use humor to de-escalate tense situations with students and staff.

Chapter 6

Where the Wild Things Learn

Where the Wild Things Grow: Leading and Learning with WILD Minds

This one's for Jamal, who never sat still a day in his life but could explain quantum mechanics after watching one TikTok.

It's for Priya, who refused to read anything unless it was manga and is now writing her own graphic novels.

It's for Aaliyah's mama, who came to every meeting with her own rubrics and once told me, "If y'all don't challenge her, I will."

It's for Mr. Novak, who plays heavy metal during independent reading time because his students said it helps them focus—and guess what? It does.

It's also for sweet Yusuf, who wrote a poem about peace after being suspended for fighting. Or Mia, who said she wanted to be a "justice lawyer" because "adults always ignore kids when they tell the truth."

Let's shout out Ruby, who argued so fiercely in favor of recess equality for the 2nd graders that we renamed a section of the playground "Ruby's Run." And Elijah, who insisted on starting a student podcast called "The Young and the Reckless" to discuss cafeteria policies and gum chewing bans.

These are the Wild Ones. The future world-builders. The change agents. The ones who don't just think outside the box—they compost it, recycle the edges, and turn it into a diorama of what school should really be.

And us? We're the leaders who stop trying to tame the wild—and start learning from it.

Education isn't about taming students—it's about guiding them. The best schools don't stifle individuality; they create space where wildness meets wisdom, where every student, teacher, parent, and leader has the freedom to grow. The challenge?

Understanding that today's non-conforming students often grow into non-conforming adults—some of whom shake up the world for the better, while others spend their days arguing with customer service reps over conspiracy theories. Our job as educators and community leaders is to steer that energy in a productive direction.

The Wild Grows With Them

That student who refuses to do group work because "no one else will do it right" grows into the coworker who emails the entire office at 11:57 p.m. with a "gentle reminder" about deadlines. The child who challenges every rule in the classroom will either become a groundbreaking entrepreneur or the person who insists on arguing with TSA about why they *should* be able to bring homemade soup through security.

Wild learners—those who resist conformity, question authority, and challenge traditional structures—don't disappear when they turn 18. They become the disruptors, the innovators, the ones who force institutions to evolve. Thank goodness for them! The problem isn't their wildness; it's that we don't always know what to do with it in school settings.

WILD Teaching: Where Structure Meets Freedom

Paulo Freire's dialogic learning reminds us that education works best when it's a conversation, not a one-way transfer of knowledge. WILD learners thrive when they are given an active role in their education, where their contributions are recognized and encouraged.

WILD Tip: Student-Led Conferences

Instead of standard parent-teacher conferences where adults talk *about* the student, have students lead the conversation. Let them discuss their progress, strengths, and areas for growth. The ability to advocate for themselves now will serve them well later—whether they're negotiating a raise or explaining to a judge why their parking ticket was a gross miscarriage of justice.

Humor: The Ultimate Leadership Strategy

There is a reason people with a great sense of humor tend to do well in leadership roles—it's the ultimate diffuser of tension, the bridge between opposing perspectives, and the fastest way to get people to actually _listen_. Around the world, effective leaders weave humor into their approach:

- United Kingdom – British school leaders use humor to humanize their role and build strong, trusting relationships with their staff. A well-timed joke can do more for morale than a thousand PowerPoint slides on "teamwork."

- South Korea – Humor is subtly woven into lessons to engage students without diminishing the respect between teachers and learners. It's proof that you can have fun _and_ maintain academic rigor.

Wildness in the Community: From Students to Citizens

The community also plays a role in fostering (or frustrating) wild learners. Schools that embrace non-conforming students can translate that support for community initiatives that give these individuals a space to thrive. How?

- Entrepreneurial Incubators in Schools – Let students with "authority issues" channel their energy into problem-solving and business creation. They may not want to follow rules, but they'll make *their own* rules if you give them the space.

- Youth Advocacy Panels – Give students a real voice in shaping school and community policies. They'll question everything anyway—why not harness that into meaningful dialogue?

- Humor-Based Mentoring – Pair students with adults who have used their nonconformity to succeed. It's one thing to be told, "You need to sit still and listen." It's another to hear from a thriving entrepreneur who says, "I was just like you, and here's how I made it work."

Embracing the WILD Means Shaping the Future

Instead of suppressing nonconformity, we should be guiding it toward innovation, leadership, and community transformation. After all, the same students who question authority today might be the ones writing the laws, leading organizations, and changing the world tomorrow. The wildness doesn't disappear—it just finds new ways to grow. Our job isn't to tame it. It's to give it direction.

If all else fails, at least we'll have some great stories to tell at retirement parties. LOL!

Conclusion
Stay WILD, Stay Free, Stay You

L isten, if you've made it this far in the book, congratulations! Either you're deeply invested in this whole "education with humor and heart" thing, or you just enjoy reading my mildly chaotic thoughts. Either way, I appreciate you.

Now let's be real for a second. The world—especially the world of education—loves a box. A neat, tiny, pre-labeled box where everyone stays where they "belong." But me? I don't do boxes. Never have, never will. I grew up in the extreme South, where people loved to tell me exactly who I should be, how I should talk, how I should act, and what dreams I should shrink down to fit inside their tiny expectations. I rejected all of that with a *quickness*.

See, when you've spent your life navigating spaces that weren't made for you, you learn a thing or two about adaptability. You learn how to read a room, how to make folks laugh when they don't know what to do with you, and how to hold your own when they decide you're "too much." You learn how to *lead*, not because you were invited to, but because you had no other choice. And most importantly, you learn that there's nothing more powerful than being fully, unapologetically seen—for your brilliance, your messiness, your magic, and your *wildness*.

That's what this whole book has been about. It's not just about leading schools, but about leading people—especially the ones who don't fit the mold—The WILD ones. The ones who challenge, question, and refuse to just go with the flow. If you've been reading this thinking, *"Whew, this sounds a little too much like me,"* then congratulations—you've got that WILD streak too. Welcome to the club.

So, what's next? Well, that's up to you. You can go back to doing things the way they've always been done, pretending that tradition is the same thing as wisdom. *Or* you can embrace what we both already know—that the real magic happens when you make space for people to be fully themselves.

Because at the end of the day, great leadership, great teaching, and great living isn't about control. It's about <u>connection</u>. It's about creating spaces where people don't have to shrink themselves to succeed. It's about seeing and being seen. It's about knowing that WILD isn't a weakness—it's a calling.

So, go on. Play your WILD card. Shake things up. Change the game, and do it all with a little humor, a whole lot of heart, and absolutely no apologies.

We weren't built for boxes; We were built to *break* them.

It is always my ultimate desire that every word I speak be for the advancement of everything related to education, and let's be honest: those of us who have been in education for a while know that we're not *just* teachers.

We are mentors, counselors, mediators, assessors! The list is astounding!

More than anything, we are called to be *facilitators*! Facilitators create opportunities and activities that help students learn *independently*.

CREATE THE RUNWAY, POINT THEM IN THE RIGHT DIRECTION, AND HELP THEM LAUNCH!

DR. VA ... signing off.

About the Author

D r. Vance-Anderson has danced through classrooms, boardrooms, and auditoriums, making her mark as an educator, leader, and advocate across the southern region of the United States, but specifically, the great state of Mississippi. From elementary scribblers to high school dreamers, she's shared in their triumphs and tears, navigating the vibrant, complex world of education with heart and humor.

Armed with a wealth of knowledge, Dr. Vance-Anderson doesn't just know her stuff—she lives it. Her groundbreaking dissertation explored "Parent Perspectives on Selecting Charter Schools for Their Special Needs Children," cementing her reputation as a passionate advocate for students of all abilities.

Her career has been a kaleidoscope of roles: College Professor, Educational Consultant, Special Education Director, Teacher, Guidance Counselor, Assistant Principal, Interim Principal, and even Technical Assistance provider for the Mississippi Department of Education. She's graced countless educational panels, tackling tough topics like transitions for students with disabilities and the social-emotional hurdles faced by learners in urban and high-poverty areas.

At home, Dr. Vance-Anderson wears her favorite titles: Mom to 4, and Wife to Adrien Anderson, a fellow educator. Whether she's transforming schools or swapping stories at the dinner table, her life's mission remains the same—nurturing minds, sparking joy, and unlocking the wild potential in every "wild child" she meets.

Dr. Vance-Anderson's debut book weaves wisdom and wit, shining a spotlight on the generational quirks, creative strategies, and delightful chaos that come with educating the brilliantly bold and wonderfully disruptive.

Appendix A

Sample Professional Development Guide: Supporting & Educating Non-conformist Students

Training Objectives:

By the end of this training, educators will be able to:

1. Identify the characteristics of a non-conformist student.

2. Understand the reasons why some students resist traditional structures.

3. Implement strategies that engage and support non-conformist students.

4. Use humor, flexibility, and creativity to manage nonconformity without losing structure.

5. Develop classroom policies that balance autonomy with accountability.

Session Outline

1. Understanding Non-conformist Students (30 minutes)

Defining Nonconformity

- Students who challenge norms without being defiant.

- Creative, independent thinkers who question authority.

- Often deeply passionate but struggle with rigid structures.

Common Traits & Behaviors

- Asking "why" frequently and challenging classroom norms.

- Disliking repetitive tasks or standard learning formats.

- Expressing themselves in unique ways (fashion, projects, humor).

- Resisting traditional authority structures but still engaging when respected.

Case Study 1: The Philosophical Challenger

Student: Caleb, a 7th grader, often interrupts history lessons to question the fairness of historical events.

Teacher Response: Instead of shutting him down, the teacher allows him to present an alternative viewpoint in a structured way (debate, research project).Outcome: Caleb remains engaged and learns to challenge ideas constructively.

2. Why Do Some Students Nonconform? (30 minutes)

5 Core Motivations:

1. Curiosity & Intellectual Stimulation – They need more depth than standard lessons provide.

2. Autonomy & Control – They thrive when given ownership of their learning.

3. Justice & Fairness – They dislike arbitrary rules and push back against injustice.

4. Passion-Driven Engagement – They learn best when connected to their interests.

5. Creative & Playful Expression – They often push boundaries as a form of humor or self-expression.

Case Study 2: The Unapologetic Individualist

Student: Sophia, a 10th grader, refuses to follow standard presentation formats, preferring spoken word poetry over PowerPoint.

Teacher Response: Instead of forcing conformity, the teacher allows creative freedom while maintaining clear expectations.Outcome: Sophia remains engaged while still meeting learning objectives.

3. Strategies for Teaching Non-conformist Students (45 minutes)

A. Classroom Strategies

- Choice-Based Assignments – Allow multiple ways to complete work.

- Encourage Debate & Inquiry – Let students challenge ideas in a structured way.

- Flexible Classroom Rules – Have clear non-negotiables but allow room for individuality.

- Student-Led Learning – Let students design projects based on their interests.

- Incorporate Humor & Playfulness – Defuse resistance with a lighthearted approach.

Case Study 3: The Absurd Rule-Challenger

Student: Marcus, a 9th grader, insists on challenging every school rule for fun.

Teacher Response: Instead of arguing, the teacher makes him write persuasive essays defending his proposed changes.Outcome: Marcus learns the value of structured arguments and critical thinking.

B. Behavior Management Strategies

- Acknowledge Their Perspective – Say *"I see your point, let's explore that."*

- Redirect, Don't Suppress – Instead of shutting down ideas, guide them into productive discussions.

- Set Boundaries With Humor – Instead of *"No, you can't question the rules"*, try *"You're welcome to start a petition after class!"*

- Use Natural Consequences – If a student insists on breaking a minor rule, let them experience the consequences in a learning-focused way.

Case Study 4: The Anti-Homework Advocate

Student: Jake, an 11th grader, refuses to do homework, arguing that "real learning happens outside of school."

Teacher Response: Instead of a power struggle, the teacher challenges Jake to create a "real-world learning" alternative assignment.

Outcome: Jake proposes a community service-based learning project, and engagement increases.

4. Practical Takeaways & Fun Educator Survival Tips (30 minutes)

A. When to Push Back & When to Let Go

- Non-Negotiable: Respect for others, participation, basic class expectations.

- Flexible: How they express learning, creative choices, challenging ideas.

- Totally Fine to Laugh About: When they bring absurd arguments (e.g., "School should have nap time").

B. Hilarious Educator Coping Strategies

- Keep a "Ridiculous Arguments" Journal – Write down the funniest rule challenges!

- Have a "Debate Day" – Let students argue outrageous points for fun (e.g., "Is cereal soup?").

- Embrace Their Energy – Some of the best future leaders are the ones who push back now.

C. Encouragement for Teachers

- Nonconformists keep classrooms exciting!

- They think differently, which is a skill we should nurture.

- One day, they will be the ones innovating, advocating, and leading change.

Appendix B

WILD Resources for Educators, Parents, and the Brave Souls Who Support Non-conforming Students (Birth to 99+)

Because let's be honest—supporting WILD students requires more than patience. It requires a strategic game plan, the ability to laugh at the madness, and a collection of resources that won't bore you to tears. So, here's a mix of practical tools, research-backed strategies, and just the right amount of humor to help you survive (and thrive) while guiding the beautifully unpredictable minds of non-conforming students.

For the Littlest WILD Ones (Ages 0-5)

Because some kids show up nonconforming straight out of the womb. If your toddler is already negotiating bedtime like a high-powered attorney, this section is for you.

Books & Guides:

- "The Explosive Child" – Dr. Ross Greene(*For when your three-year-old refuses to wear pants because of "sensory oppression."*)

- "Raising Your Spirited Child" – Mary Sheedy Kurcinka(*A survival guide for parents of kids who feel EVERYTHING at a level 10.*)

- "No Bad Kids: Toddler Discipline Without Shame" – Janet Lansbury(*Because telling a toddler "just stop" is as effective as telling a cat to take a bath.*)

Resources & Strategies:

- Child-Led Play Therapy – Let them process their emotions through dramatic reenactments. (Warning: You will be assigned a role. You may or may not be the villain.)

- Songs that Teach Social-Emotional Skills – "Daniel Tiger's Neighborhood" is basically therapy for toddlers in song form. Accept it.

- The Toddler's Bill of Rights (Unofficial) – 1) The floor is lava, 2) Pants are optional, 3) "Because I said so" is NOT a real answer.

Elementary School WILD Cards (Ages 6-12)

Where they master loopholes, develop strong opinions on injustice, and somehow learn to argue like seasoned debaters.

Books & Guides:

- "The Whole-Brain Child" – Dr. Dan Siegel & Tina Payne Bryson(*Because you need to understand their brains before they overthrow your household/classroom.*)

- "How to Talk So Kids Will Listen & Listen So Kids Will Talk" – Adele Faber & Elaine Mazlish(*For when "BECAUSE I SAID SO" no longer works.*)

- "Grit" – Angela Duckworth(*Because sometimes the most stubborn kids turn into the most resilient adults.*)

Resources & Strategies:

- Choice Boards & Flexible Learning Spaces – Let them pick their own way of doing things. If they're going to resist, might as well make them feel like they *chose* the resistance.

- Role-Playing Conflict Resolution – Teach them to navigate life's challenges by pretending to be pirates, astronauts, or reality TV contestants.

- Global Pen Pal Programs – Because sometimes they need to see that other kids across the world are just as wild and wonderful.

The Middle School WILD Era (Ages 12-14)

Otherwise known as "The Unfiltered Opinion & Mismatched Outfit Years." Approach with caution and snacks.

Books & Guides:

"Untangled: Guiding Teenage Girls Through the Seven Transitions Into Adulthood" – Lisa Damour(*Because sometimes tween emotions hit harder than reality TV plot twists.*)

"The Teenage Brain" – Frances Jensen(*So you can scientifically prove they're not just ignoring you for fun—well, mostly.*)

"Middle School: The Worst Years of My Life" – James Patterson(*Because if they won't listen to you, at least they might listen to a funny book about their struggles.*)

Resources & Strategies:

- Genius Hour Projects – Let them research something they love. Even if it's *conspiracy theories about whether birds are government drones.*

- Music-Based Learning – The right playlist can make any lesson less painful. (Yes, even algebra.)

- "Roast & Reflect" Sessions – A safe space where they can vent, but then problem-solve like a boss. (Warning: They will absolutely roast you too. Stay strong.)

High School & Beyond WILD (Ages 15-18+)

At this point, they either want to change the world or just want you to stop talking. Either way, they're moving fast.

Books & Guides:

- "Daring Greatly" – Brené Brown(*Because vulnerability isn't just for emotional TED Talks—it's also a leadership skill.*)

- "The 5 Second Rule" – Mel Robbins(*For when they need a simple trick to overcome procrastination. Because waiting for motivation isn't working.*)

- "Atomic Habits" – James Clear(*Because "I'll do it later" is their official motto, and this book helps.*)

Resources & Strategies:

- YouTube University & Skillshare – If they want to learn it, they'll Google it. Encourage self-directed learning with actual structure.

- Entrepreneurial Incubators & Internship Programs – Let them build something real. Even if it's just a TikTok side hustle.

- Improv & Debate Clubs – They love arguing? Good. Teach them to argue *strategically*—and make it work for them.

For the WILD Adults (Ages 18-99+)

Because nonconformists don't magically "settle down" after high school. If anything, they just get louder and funnier.

Books & Guides:

- "You Are a Badass" – Jen Sincero(*Because sometimes adults need permission to embrace their WILD side too.*)

- "The Subtle Art of Not Giving a F*"** – Mark Manson(*For those who need a little help choosing their battles—and their joy.*)

- "Big Magic" – Elizabeth Gilbert(*Because creativity is not a phase—it's survival.*)

Resources & Strategies:

- Book Clubs for WILD Minds – Find your people. The ones who still question everything and laugh too loud in public.

- Public Speaking & Storytelling Workshops – You've got stories. The world needs to hear them.

- Travel & Cross-Cultural Experiences – The best way to keep your mind WILD? Go see the world. (And don't just stay in the tourist spots.)

Resources Are Great, But So Are You.

At the end of the day, no book, website, or strategy can replace being present, listening, and creating space for people to be fully themselves. Whether you're guiding a tiny toddler or a rebellious teenager—or figuring out how to keep your *own* WILD self-thriving—just remember:

WILD is not a weakness—it's a superpower. If you don't laugh, you'll cry—so choose laughter. The world needs more disruptors, questioners, and creative minds!

So go forth, play your WILD card, and make some magic. And if you mess up? Well... that's just part of the adventure.

References

Covey, S. (1989). *The 7 habits of highly effective people.* Free Press.

Dewey, J. (1938). *Experience and education.* Macmillan.

Dweck, C. (2006). *Mindset: The new psychology of success.* Random House.

Epstein, J. (2009). *School, family, and community partnerships.* Westview Press.

Freire, P. (1970). *Pedagogy of the oppressed.* Herder and Herder.

Gardner, H. (1983). *Frames of mind: The theory of multiple intelligences.* Basic Books.

Maslow, A. H. (1943). *A theory of human motivation.* Psychological Review, 50(4), 370–396.

Robinson, K. (2006). *Do schools kill creativity?* [TED Talk]. TED Conferences.

Silberman, S. (2015). *NeuroTribes: The legacy of autism and the future of WILD.* Avery.

Vygotsky, L. (1978). *Mind in society.* Harvard University Press.

www.ingramcontent.com/pod-product-compliance
Lightning Source LLC
Chambersburg PA
CBHW061703120626
46550CB00003B/1071